Michael McClure
Selected Poems

D1483784

ALSO BY MICHAEL McCLURE

Michael McClure
Selected Poems

A New Directions Book

The poems in this volume have been selected from the following books by Michael McClure: *Hymns to Saint Geryon* (The Auerhahn Press, 1959; reissued by Grey Fox Press, 1980), *The New Book / A Book of Torture* (Grove Press, 1961), *Little Odes* (Black Sparrow Press, 1969), *Star* (Grove Press, 1970), *Rare Angel* (Black Sparrow Press, 1974), *September Blackberries* (New Directions, 1974), *Jaguar Skies* (New Directions, 1975), *Antechamber & Other Poems* (New Directions, 1978), and *Fragments of Perseus* (New Directions, 1983).

Manufactured in the United States of America
First published clothbound and as New Directions Paperbook 599 in 1986
Published simultaneously in Canada by Penguin Books Canada Limited

Library of Congress Cataloging-in-Publication Data
McClure, Michael.
  Selected poems.
  (A New Directions Book)
  I. Title.
PS3563.A262A6   1986   811'.54   85–21477
ISBN 0–8112–0950–4
ISBN 0–8112–0951–2 (pbk.)

New Directions Books are published for James Laughlin
by New Directions Publishing Corporation,
80 Eighth Avenue, New York 10011

CONTENTS

AUTHOR'S NOTE

These poems are selected intuitively—not only as some of my best poems but ones that please me and I hope you also. They follow one vibration or band of artistic consciousness like a path or set of stepping stones. This selection is like one arrow from a quiver from which I might have drawn others. These poems deal with the poem as organism, and with biology and with the love that we invent. Mostly they are short poems and poems of middle length. To balance that, the opening of a long poem, *Rare Angel,* is included. I have not excerpted sections from other poems of length, such as *Xes* or *Dark Brown,* because each should be read as a whole. The beast language stanzas in *Ghost Tantras* are not represented here because they would be a distraction in a sampler of my verse. I hope they will have readers on their own terms.

Except for *Rare Angel* the poems are in chronological order. There are few changes in the writing. The deliberate personalizations of grammar, and alterations of accepted written syntax, are for me like the splashings of paint in modern canvases. I continue to see the poem as an extension of myself, as a gesture, and as an organism seeking life.

—Michael McClure

Rise, like lions after slumber,
In unvanquishable number,
Shake your chains to earth like dew
Which in sleep had fall'n on you

Michael McClure
Selected Poems

NIGHT WORDS: THE RAVISHING

How beautiful things are in a beautiful room
At night
Without proportion
A black longhaired cat with a sensitive human face
A white robe hangs on the wall
Like a soft ghost
Without proportion
Songs flit through my head
The room is calm and still and cool
Blue gray stillness
Without proportion
The plants are alive
Giving off votive oxygen
To the benevolent pictures above them
Songs flit through my head
I am taken with insomnia
With ambrosial insomnia
And songs flit through my head
The room is softened
Things are without proportion
And I must sleep

THE MYSTERY OF THE HUNT

It's the mystery of the hunt that intrigues me,
That drives us like lemmings, but cautiously—
The search for a bright square cloud—the scent of lemon
[verbena—
Or to learn rules for the game the sea otters
Play in the surf.

It is these small things—and the secret behind them
That fill the heart.
The pattern, the spirit, the fiery demon
That link them together
And pull their freedom into our senses,

The smell of a shrub, a cloud, the action of animals

—The rising, the exuberance, when the mystery is unveiled.
It is these small things

That when brought into vision become an inferno.

FOR THE DEATH OF 100 WHALES

*". . . Killer whales . . . Savage sea cannibals up to 30 feet long with
teeth like bayonets . . . one was caught with 14 seals and 13 porpoises
in its belly . . . often tear at boats and nets . . . destroyed thousands of
dollars worth of fishing tackle . . . Icelandic government appealed to
the U.S., which has thousands of men stationed at a lonely NATO
airbase on the subarctic island. Seventy-nine bored G.I.'s responded
with enthusiasm. Armed with rifles and machine guns one posse of
Americans climbed into four small boats and in one morning wiped
out a pack of 100 killers . . .*

*". . . First the killers were rounded up into tight formation with
concentrated machine gun fire, then moved out again one by one, for
the final blast which would kill them . . . as one was wounded, the
others would set upon it and tear it to pieces with their jagged
teeth . . ."*

TIME, *April 1954*

Hung midsea
Like a boat mid-air
The Liners boiled their pastures:
The Liners of flesh,
The Arctic steamers.

Brains the size of a football.
Mouths the size of a door.

The sleek wolves
Mowers and reapers of sea kine.
THE GIANT TADPOLES
(Meat their algae)
Lept
Like sheep or children.
Shot from the sea's bore.
Turned and twisted
(Goya!!)
Flung blood and sperm.

3

Incense.
Gnashed at their tails and brothers,
Cursed Christ of mammals,
Snapped at the sun,
Ran for the sea's floor.

Goya! Goya!
Oh Lawrence,
No angels dance those bridges.
OH GUN! OH BOW!
There are no churches in the waves,
No holiness,
No passages or crossings
From the beasts' wet shore.

THE ROBE

Sleepwalkers . . . Ghosts! Voices
like bodies coming through the mists of sleep,
we float about each other—

bare feet not touching the floor.
Talking in our lover's voice
NAMING THE OBJECTS OF LOVE

(Inventing new tortures,
machines to carry us.
Wonders full blown in our faces.
Eyes like sapphires or opals.
Aloof as miracles. Hearing
jazz in the air. We are passing—

our shapes like nasturtiums.)
Frozen, caught, held there

my shoulders won't hold you.

HEROIC ACTS
won't free us. Free us. Love.
We are voices. Sleep is with us.

HYMN TO SAINT GERYON

THE GESTURE THE GESTURE THE GESTURE THE GES-
                              [TURE THE GESTURE THE
GESTURE THE GESTURE   to make fists of it.

Clyfford Still: "We are committed to an unqualified act,
not illustrating outworn myths or contemporary alibis. One must
accept total responsibility for what he executes.
And the measure of his greatness will be the depth of his
insight and courage in realizing
his own vision. Demands for communication are pre-
sumptuous and irrelevant."

To hit with the thing. To make a robe of it
TO WEAR.
To fill out the thing as we see it!
To clothe ourselves in the action,
to remove from the precious to the full swing.
To hit the object over the head. To step
into what we conjecture.
Name it the *stance*. Not politics

but ourselves—is the question.
HERE I SEE IT WITH FLOWERS ENTERING INTO IT

that way.
Not caring except for my greatness, caring
only for my size I would enter it.

THE SELFS FREE HERO

THOREAU is there, LAWRENCE, BLAKE and GOYA
ST. POLLOCK is there and KLINE whom I imagine
in a world of nerves and nightsweats.
To hit it again. "The foot is to kick with."

6

If I do violence to myself I am beautiful, blood is red
on the face and bruises are not without . . .

But the thing I say!! Is to see

Or as one says: Not to lie about goodness.
Even Geryon (as Geryon) is beautiful but not if you look
only at the head or body. BUT

BACK TO IT . . . it is a robe
that I want. The gestures that we make are
our clothing. Small gestures
are like smoke, a slight breeze causes a drifting
and we are bare again . . . uneternal.
Say it! What a small thing to want, it is not
noble. Shelley wanted to save the Irish.
But I love my body my face only
first and then others'.
To fill out a vision until I become
one with it. Or perhaps both happen together. But
I must be an animal. Shelley had
no gods either.   ....
An impetuous man—he was mostly
Gesture!!!!!!!!!!!!
There are so few poems
but so much of him.
AND I COULD BE FORCED BY SOMEONE TO CHANGE
                                                      [THIS

THEY WOULD KNOW THAT WHAT I SAY IS NOT
                              [MEANT AS HUMOR

Or to
STRIKE THEM
with the
GESTURE.

7

I mean that I love myself which is an act of pride
and I would decorate myself with what is beautiful.
The tygers of wrath are wiser than the horses of instruction—
means that the belief of something is necessary to its beauty.
Size, numbers are part of any esthetic. I must
believe my gesture. Beauty fades so quickly

that it does not matter. Belief, pride—remain.
AND   AND   AND   AND   AND   AND   AND   AND

the gesture.
The mark of the strong shoulder and hand.

•

Yes, confuses. The whole thing.
Sometimes intentional and sometimes out of my hands.
Robe Gesture   ROBE/GESTURE   Robe Gesture
The poem like painting is black and white.

•

And I am still not swinging it—there is still confusion
I PICK IT UP BY THE TAIL AND HIT
YOU OVER THE HEAD WITH IT.

8

WHAP WHAP WHAP WHAP WHAP WHAP WHAP WHAP
[WHAP
DO YOU BELIEVE ME NOW?

No. But if I started huge paragraphs moving toward you
or enormous stanzas, simple things, part of
a gesture, then, you would get out of the way.
You would see them coming at you,
rapidly, determined, indifferent. But this
is really not to attack you.
I mean only to move words. To set
something into motion toward a goal. Not
to invent new confusions.

It is hard to avoid some issues.
The poem could easily become a body
with elbows, lymph systems, muscles.
But how ugly! How much better for it

to be a body of words.
A POEM—NO MORE
(Not a body of words but a poem)

I am the body, the animal, the poem
is a gesture of mine.

A confusion is avoided here,

Beauty: How beautiful I move
and make gestures. How
beautiful that sometimes I believe in them.
Sometimes I make a strong gesture—a poem
and I record it.

9

ODE TO JACKSON POLLOCK

Hand swinging the loops of paint—splashes—drips—
chic lavender, *duende* black, blue and red!

Jackson Pollock my sorrow is selfish. I won't meet
you here. I see your crossings of paint!
We are all lost in the cloud of our gestures—

—the smoke we make with our arms. I cry
to my beloved too. We are lost
in lovelessness. Our sorrows
before us. Copy them in air! We
make their postures with our stance.

They grow before us.
The lean black she-wolves on altars of color.
We search our remembrance for memories
of heroic anguish. We put down
our pain as singing testimony.
Gouges, corruptions, wrinkles, held loose

in the net of our feelings and hues—
we crash into their machinery making it
as we believe. I say

we. I—You. You saw the brightness
of pain. Ambition. We give in to the lie
of beauty in the step of creating.
Make lies to live in. I mean you. Held
yourself in animal suffering.
You made your history. Of Pain.

Making it real for beauty, for ambition
and power. Invented totems from teacups
and cigarettes. Put it all down

in disbelief—waiting—forcing.
Each gesture painting. —Caught on
to the method of making each motion
your speech, your love, your rack

and found yourself. Heroic—huge—burning
with your feelings. Like making money
makes the body move. Calls you to action
swirling the paint and studying the feeling

caught up in the struggle and leading it.
For the beauty of animal action
and freedom of full reward.
To see it down—and praise—and admiration,
to lead, to feel yourself above all others.

NO MATTER WHAT—IT'S THERE! NO ONE

can remove it. Done in full power.
Liberty and Jackson Pollock the creator.
The mind is given credit.

You strangled
the lean wolf beloved to yourself—
Guardians of the Secret
—and found yourself the secret
spread in clouds of color

burning yourself and falling like rain

transmuted into grace and glory, free
of innocence

containing all, pressing experience
through yourself onto the canvas.
Pollock I know you are there! Pollock
do you hear me? !! Spoke to himself

beloved. As I speak to myself
to Pollock into the air. And fall short

of the body of the beloved hovering
always before him. Her face
not a fact, memory or experience
but there in the air
destroying confidence.
The enormous figure of her mystery

always there in trappings of reason.

Worked at his sureness. Demanding
Her place beside him. Called

from the whirls of paint, asked for
a face and shoulders to stand naked
before him to make a star.

He pulling the torn parts of her body
together
to make a perfect figure—1951.
Assembled the lovely shape of chaos.
Seeing it bare and hideous, new
to the old eye. Stark
black and white. The perfect figure
lying in it peering from it.
And he gave her what limbs and lovely face
he could
from the squares, angles, loops, splashes, broken shapes
he saw of all with bare eye and body.

ODE FOR SOFT VOICE

for Joanna

And sometimes in the cool night I see you are an animal
LIKE NO OTHER AND HAVE AS STRANGE A SCENT AS
[ANY AND MY BREATH AND
energy go out to you.
And see love as an invention and play it extemporaneously.

And I who cannot love can love you.
OH THIS THIS THIS IS THE HURT/THAT WE DO NOT
[KICK
down the walls and do not see them.
And I do not ache until I scent you. And I
do not scent you. Breathing moves us. Breath is . . .

And more than this that we are huge and clear
and open—locked inside
and moving out and we make outlines in the air the shapes
they are. And we shift so. We move and never keep our forms but
[stare
at them address them as if they were there. This is my hand with
5 fingers, my heart nerves lungs
are there and part of me
and I move.
I have no form but lies and drop them from me.

I am a shape and meet you
at our skins' edge.
We change and speak and make our histories. I am all I feel
and what you see and what you touch.
There are no walls but ones we make.
I AM SICK CONFUSED AND DROP IT FROM ME.
The nerves are dead that feel no hunger or pain there's no tri-
umph but failure. This is the last speech of seraphim or beast sick

13

in need for change and chaos. The room of banished love for beauty. The tooth in our breast. What we see is real and able to our hand, what we feel is beauty (BEAUTY) what we strike is hatred, what we scent is odorous. This about me is my bride if I kick aside the forms of it for woman world and mineral for air for earth for fire and water for table chair and blood.

LA PLUS BLANCHE

JEAN HARLOW, YOU ARE IN BEAUTY ON DARK
                [EARTH WITH WHITE FEET! MICHAEL
slaying the dragon is not more wonderful than you. To air
you give magical sleekness. We shall carry you into Space
on our shoulders. You triumph over all with warm legs and a
smile of wistful anxiety that's cover for the honesty
spoken by your grace! Inner energy presses out to you in
                                [warmness—

you return love. Love returned for admiration! Strangeness
is returned by you for desire. How. Where
but in the depth of Jean Harlow is such strangeness
made into grace? How many women are more beautiful
in shape and apparition! How few can /have/

draw such love to them? For you are the whole creature of love!

Your muscles are love muscles!

Your nerves—Love nerves!

And your upturned
comic eyes!
Sleep dreams of you.

15

MAD SONNET

THE PLUMES OF LOVE ARE BLACK! THE PLUMES OF
[LOVE ARE BLACK
AND DELICATE!   OH!
and shine like moron-eyed plumes of a peacock
with violetshine and yellow on shadowy black.
They spray SPRAY from the body of the Beloved. Vanes shaking
[in air!

AND I DO NOT WANT BLACK PLUMES OR AGONY . . .
[AND I DO
NOT SURRENDER. And I ask for noble combat!!
to give pure Love
as best I can
with opened heart
LOVE!!
I have not seen you before and you're
more beautiful than a plume!

Stately, striding in Space and warm . . . (Your
human breasts!)
LET ME MAKE YOUR SMILE AND HEARTSHAPED
[FACE IMMORTAL

- -

YOUR GRAY EYES ARE WHAT I FINALLY COME TO
[WITH MY BROWN!
AND YOUR HIGH CHEEKS, and your hair rough
for a woman's—like a lamb. And the walking Virtue
that you are!

ODE

The Love and VISION of the Instant are the venom we coil
our tiny bodies on. I am this sensual!
I AM THIS SIZE!! I AM THIS SIZE
AND THERE IS NO OTHER AS WE LIE COILED
in the black lily of our lives.
The instant is the giant lamp we throw
our shadows by. I love you honeyed venom.
The instant is without thorn and I cannot be
hung on it
the instant is not rose but lily
and we may be fairy creatures
HUGER THAN THE STARS!!!

BREAK DOWN THE STINKING SWEAT OF FEAR
that rises in my nose like flames!

NOT THE UGLY PLAIN SPEECH AMONG THE REAL
[SCULPTURES
OF THE REAL
HELL AND UGLINESS but the soft warmth of eternal
[imagination
and delicate beauty. Rise to me from your blossom instant
make new capitals and smash the old. Ignore the falsity
and

17

HUMMINGBIRD ODE

THE FAR-DARTER IS DEAD IN MY HAND, THE
[BEAUTIFUL
SHABBY COLORS!!
and the damp spots where the eyes were. Small form
that was all spirit, smashed on the plate
glass window. The green head and ruby
ruffles. The beautiful shabby colors
and the damp spots where the eyes were.
All head and chest and the Eros-spear
of the beak. Moving like Cupid
in the fuschias.
Hummingbird and spike of desire.

The huge chest and head and the beautiful
shabby colors. Tiny legs
thrust back in the last stiff agony.

WHAT'S
ON YOUR SIDE OF THE VEIL??
DO YOU DIP YOUR BEAK
in the vast black lily
of space? Does the sweetness
of the pain go on forever?

IS THERE COURAGE THERE IN THE NIGHT?
WHERE ARE THE LOVES THAT MAKE THE BLOSSOM
of your body? Do they still spin
in the air? Your wives
and loves? Are you now
more than this meat? Finally
A STAR??

ON BEGINNING ROMEO AND JULIET

"Adding to clouds more clouds with his deep sighs . . ." then let
[him
think on love! ADDING LOVE TO LOVE himself becoming
smoke burning the blossom incense of his meat.
Crave love, and add love to love, walk in deep
night, make sighs, let tears fall in full
knowledge of what few men
know, or feel at his age.
AND LET HIM DIE THEN!
With momentary love never torn
by bestial teeth of others
from his womblike soul.
And let him die like Mercutio's

Grecian merriment not far (in days)
from his ears!! What ever could
he hope for better? To die
with memories of robust men
and blood. (And Juliet's soft white
childlike heavenly beauty

still tastewise on his lips and fin-
gertips!)

TO BE A PROUD MURDERER AND LOVER

A CHILD COUPLED TO A CHILD

THE SIGH AND MEAT OF SIGH !

Oh, add them for they are clear smokey perfume

19

COLD SATURDAY MAD SONNET

ON COLD SATURDAY I WALKED IN THE EMPTY
[VALLEY OF WALL STREET.
I dreamed with the hanging concrete eagles
and I spoke with the black-bronze foot of Washington.
I strode in the vibrations
of money-strength
in the narrow, cold, lovely CHASM.

Oh perfect chill slot of space!

WALL STREET, WALL STREET,
MOUNTED WITH DEAD BEASTS AND MEN
and metal placards greened and darkened.
AND A CATHEDRAL AT YOUR HEAD!

- -

I see that the men are alive and born
and inspired
by the moving beauty of their (own) physical figures
who will tear
the vibrations-of-strength from the vibrations-of-money
and drop them like a dollar on the chests
of the Senate!
They step with the pride of a continent.

VALENTINE'S DAY SONNET

GLORIOUS DIVINE CREATURE, I'VE JUST SEEN YOUR
[NAKEDNESS,
your womanly-muscled flesh, and lambliness again
in new light.
I SMELL THE SULFUR AND SPRUCE
in your hair. And the dream-scent of your sleek waist.

But it is the relaxed light upon your brow and cheeks
that tells me
YOU MUST BE PROTECTED
from Rippers and Devourers. (They seek
at random gentle beings for torment.
How you must drive them mad!) You smile
simply from reality in back of dreams.
You peer from the soft cliffs into green waves
and make rippling profiles of beauty
everywhere.
WHAT STRANGE THINGS YOU SEE.

I will protect you—for now I know the secret!
Your breasts and lower belly are masters of the science
of higher thought. Your hair and lips belong to a stream
of divinity.
I shall keep your liberation safe!

21

THE SURGE

for Brakhage

    This is the failure of an attempt to write a beautiful poem.
I would like to have it looked at as the mindless coiling of a
protein that has not fully achieved life—but one that is, or might
be, a step towards living-being.

THE SURGE! THE SURGE! THE SURGE!
IT IS THE SURGE OF LIFE
I SEEK
TO VIEW . . .

Plato and Darwin are the dead heads of glorious vision.

Dante turned to the woman Beatrice
in Paradiso and she spoke:
"Tis true that oftentimes the shape
will fail to harmonize with the design
when the material is deaf to answer.
Then from its course the creature deviates;
For though impelled towards the highest heaven
it has the power to bend in other ways—
just as when fire is seen to fall from clouds
if the first impulse of its natural bent,
turned by false pleasure, drives it to the earth.
—No more, if I judge rightly,
shouldst thou marvel
at thy ascent, than at a falling rill
that plunges from the mountain to the depths.
Twould be as strange, hadst thou stayed down below . . ."

IS NOT THE OLD MALE BEAST SIGHT OF IT
as dead as Hell?

Our view of Life is still so young and so worn
and ripped by the brutal tatters we made of it!
Subtle Plato and Darwin opened worlds to us by stating
what we knew and our admissions threw us into
reality! How blind is blind?
How deaf and dumb is our dumbness? If we admit,
we do have fresher eyes. There's a calm inertness
of joy that living beings drift to and from. (And it is far
back when the Universe began . . .
and it is here now too.) I do not mean the mystic's view.
Or that of a man locked in the superstition of his own repression.
Not emotive analogies!
I mean there is a more total view!
It shifts and changes and wavers,
and weakens as our nerves do, to finally make
a greater field and more total sight.
We yearn for it . . .

I love you is the key.

The Surge of Life may not be seen by male or female
for both are halves. But perhaps the female,
who is unprincipled, sees farther and into more.

2.

OH, HOW I HAVE BEAT MY HEAD AT IT in male stupidity!
And here . . . here in my hand, is a picture of the living Universe
made by a woman as gift of love in a casual moment!
—A valentine in ballpoint ink. The drawing calls all
previous images to abeyance. The dark and radiant
swirlings in my head seem clumsy—tho I trust them too.
It is a tree that is not a tree.
It might be a placenta with thin branches or veins.

23

The stalk of it narrows to a gasp of life
and stretches downward and spreads into what
might be the earth or the top of another tree.
((Is there a forest?))
(Upon the lower treetop, or earth, lies a creature coiled
and incomplete, with round and staring eyes.)
Intersecting the narrow trunk, or crossing it, in
mysterious geometry, is a palette shape.
Upon it spins around and round, before ascending
up the stalk into the boughs, a creature that
is a ring of meat divided into the individuals
comprising it. They are hot upon each other's
tails. They stare after one another and outwards
with round eyes. Some beasts of the ring
are dots and blobs or teardrops of primal meat.
And some are more whole creatures. Some contain
within themselves, midway, an extra pair of eyes
to show their division is not complete. (Or
to assert the meaninglessness of all division
that is based on eyes or other organs.) Those eyes
deny that a single head or set of senses divide
lives in a greater sense. *The ring is one!*
The creatures
swell, spring free, and dart up the cincture
to a greater space above.

A long, large, snake-shaped molecule of flesh
coils from the earth
around the palette and caresses the higher branch
in sensuality.
The high part is a heart! Within it a man's head & shoulders
rise from a bat-winged heart with thready tail—
and a heart upon the thread tip. Nearby is a circle
(a vacuole? a nucleus?) with a shape inside that might
be any living thing from a vulture to a child.

24

High and low outside are stars that are
living sparks or moths.
Turned upside down the drawing means
not more nor less. It is a gentle
tensile surge
a woman views.

3.

Yes, all things flow! And in our male insistency on meaning
we miss the truth. The mountains do pour, moving in millionic
ripples over thousand aeons. Demanding brute reality we forget
the greater flow and then the black immediate is larger—and it is
and isn't. But Life, THE PLASM, does not flow like lead does.
It SURGES! Is that the difference?—And it is one great whole
and isn't. It is something sweeter than we see—we must feel
and hear it too! Male and female have, and do not have, im-
[portance.
They matter! *It is not relative but real!*
In black immediate I feel the roaring meat mountain
herds of Bison and of Whales or Men or solid
American clouds of birds 100 years ago.
Then I am moved by meanings and sights of
the smaller surge! Then I, dreaming,
partake in the surge like a Plains Indian
on horseback and I know my smallest gene
particles are forever spread and immortal. Distances
and hallucinations then can cause no fear;
life is primitive and acceptable.

Is all life a vast chromosome stretched in Time?
Simply a pattern for another thing?
But the pattern like the chromosomes *is* the Life,
and the Surge is its vehicle.

It does not matter!

25

It is the athletic living thing of energy!

All else is *soundless and sightless* pouring.

There is no teleology but
surging freedom.

Inert matters pour in and out of the Surge
and make sound and sight. But neither
they nor the Surge will wait. It is another matter.
Space/Space/Space is a black lily holding the rosy,
full, flowing, and everspreading and con-
tracting, spilling flash.

The woman's easy sight of it can be bolder than the man's.
She admits that we can never know, and tells
us that the question is useless words.
The Surge can never see itself for the Surge is
its self-sight. And its sight
and being are simultaneous.
There is no urge to see or feel—for it *is* sight
and feeling.

Except for the glory

GLORY

GLORY

GLORY

GLORY

GLORY

GLORY

it does not matter.

26

4.

But desire to know and feel are not eased!
To feel the caves of body and the separate
physical tug of each desire is insanity. The key
is love
and yearning. The cold sea beasts
and mindless creatures are the holders of vastest
Philosophy.
We can never touch it.
We are blessed.

Praise to the Surge of life that there is no answer
—and no question!

Genetics and memory

are the same

they are degrees of one

molecular unity.

We are bulks of revolt and systems of love-structuring
in a greater whole
beginning where the atoms come
to move together and make a coiling string . . .

Beyond the barrier
all things are laid upon a solid
and at rest.

Beatrice! Beatrice! *Paradiso is opening.*

WE ARE AT THE GATES OF THE CHERUBIC!

27

NOT YOUTH

IT IS NOT YOUTH THAT INTRIGUES ME
BUT SUPPLENESS.
The sensitivity of meat to meat and to nerve
dies with the nets of self-image.
THE SELF BECOMES RIGID
and does not open
AND EXTEND.
The structure
is frozen and rusts
like armor. Spring comes
and goes
with buds and creatures.

WE LOOK INTO A VISION
and only see
it narrowing. Beyond
that
there is a mystery
in this life like a candle flame
AND

it is moving.

I would be as perfect as a moth.

GRAY FOX AT SOLSTICE

WAVES CRASH AND FLUFF JEWEL SAND
in blackness. Ten feet from his den
the gray fox shits on the cliff edge
enjoying the beat of starlight
on his brow, and ocean
on his eardrums. The yearling
deer watches—trembling.
The fox's garden trails
down the precipice:
ice plant, wild strawberries,
succulents.
Squid eggs
in jelly bags (with moving
embryos) wash up on
the strand.
It is the night of the solstice.
The fox coughs,
"Hahh!"
Kicks his feet—
stretches.
Beautiful claw toes
in purple brodiaea lilies.
He dance-runs through
the Indian paintbrush.
Galaxies in spirals.
Galaxies in balls.
Near stars and white mist swirling.

OVER THE LEFT SHOULDER, MR.

for Dennis Hopper

THE BLUE-BLACK CLOUD COVERS THE CHIN
—A SPARKLING GREEN AURA SHOOTS
from the head. There is the smell
of civet and roses. I fill
with esthetic pleasure. THE WAR
takes place somewhere over
the left shoulder.
Happens some place
several thousand miles
away . . .

((((THERE IS A CLOUD OF A MILLION
DEAD ASIANS—BUT
it is over the left shoulder
as
somewhere near my feet psychopathic
killers high on acid—like
a cancer in eternity—kill
a pregnant movie star. SCREAMS,
PLEADINGS, SHRIEKS,
GIANT
FIGURES,
tiny like memories of this
instant . . .))))

and
we
smile
speaking
of the future
and of hope. WE

ARE HOPE FULL!

30

FOR JANE

THE YOUNG LADY CAT (TIGER TABBY)
sits, paws folded
under breast,
on green grass
in the cool
summer morning
haze
listening
to
families
of
pigeons
and
a
Vivaldi
concerto.
Very
pleased
to
be.

31

FROM THE BOOK OF JOANNA

JOANNA, YOU'RE BAD! YES,
YOU'RE ROMANCE!
I won't pat your arm again BUT
I'll remember all the pain
and beauty
that we've known together.
How your body is a little girl's.
FACE
WITH
WRINKLES
that
I've
grown with—and I love.
And yes, they're sexual—
as you are and
you know.
Sure
we've ripped at each other.
We've invented ugly little Hells.
(Though I'd rather be in one with you
than in Heaven with another.)
We've made some Heavens too, like wafting
feathers in the pillow or the air beside
the fire—or on a balcony in Paris—
or a sportscar in the desert underneath the moon
—or swimming in an icy ocean like we come together.
AND
I'VE
HEARD
YOU SHOUT
SO OFTEN
with sexuality
in full pleasure! ! !

(Do you remember? Sure
getting old is getting
old. WE'VE
GOT
FAR
TO
GO

and you're still so BLACK.

I love your toes and breasts

and butt and shoulders

and your winsome smile and all

the trails and veils of romance floating from you

when you walk.

FOR
YOU
ARE

MY

QUEEN
OF PLEASURE

and
if there's darkness in me
then your demon reflects it back

TO SOMETIMES MAKE AN ANGEL

33

and sometimes make a blessing in the guise

of fangy wolf

FOR

only you

can sometimes

let me know SHEER LOVELINESS

and only I can be your dark and fumbling guide

TO A GOLDEN LION MARMOSET

an endangered primate species

OH BEAUTIFUL LITTLE FACE,
PEERING THROUGH
THE DAWN
OF TIME,
THE GOLDEN FUR UPON YOUR CHEEKS
is precious as a rhyme.
The April in your gracious snarl
can loose a body to ungnarl
and
stand
upright in the sun.
Come back, I've caught my mind!
Your life is all I find
to prove ours are worthwhile.

The monster caterpillars
and the teeth of fire
that eat your jungle
crunch my house.
ALL
BEASTS
ARE
MEN;
all men are beasts.

BUT
I want you alive
in more than memory!

SESTINA

THE BEAUTIFUL LINES OF FLAMES IDENTIFY MY
[HEADACHE.
The fires are blue and gold and orange and turquoise.
They ring like one beat of a drum within my skull.
My being is overwhelmed by experience.
Wings grow out of my skull to fly me away to soft moss
where there is a cliff I would lie on among blossoms.

Those things that are the world are white blossoms.
They fall on the dark floor in the patterns of headache
creating a carpet in our being like moss.
From a distance the face becomes a mask of turquoise,
or jade, and it begins to reject the experience
of anything, even gentleness, that touches the skull.

I would speak with my body but my skull
is there like a crab shell decked with blossoms
and I wish to resist all but the drabbest experience
for I am lost and pounding the walls of my headache.
It is a pleasure to run fingers over turquoise.
The veins and striations may be felt as moss.

The elegance of stones is like green moss
growing on a jawbone dropped from a sheep skull
on a cliffbank in Iceland where Indian turquoise
is more exotic than these strange blossoms
that make up a constellation I call my headache.
The substrate suffers an overdose of experience.

I take notes on the body of experience
which grows as obsidian boulders and moss
and becomes, at last, the statement of headache
that vibrates minute beacons in my skull.
Each being grows unique among blossoms
of emanated gods and katydids in a field of turquoise.

36

My house is electric blue not turquoise
but I will imagine the bulks of all experience,
for, imagined or real, they are brother blossoms.
I will not regret either needles or moss.
Regardless of the noise in my skull
I will fall divinely in love with my headache.

The night might be turquoise or a pale moss
but it is all experience to be stored in the skull.
This body is made of blossoms—even my headache.

A BREATH

HOW
SWEET
TO
BE
A
ROSE
BY
CANDLE
LIGHT
or
a
worm
by
full
moon.
See the hop-
ping flight
a cricket makes.
Nature loves
the absence of
mistakes.

DEAR JANE

LIFE IS A CURTAIN
drawn across
the past
that
we know
and yet
forget.
We're
enchanted
by the fit
of silk
and glow
of melodies.
HOW
GLAD
WE ARE
to have you here
to walk beside
where the sound
of car crash
and the bird song
from the redwood
and the avocado trees
are a kind of tide
upon the breeze.

¡EL CERRO ES NUESTRO!

THE FLAME IS OURS!
We are the candle
that holds itself
aloft.
We are the Andes
among creatures
and our hands are soft
and our cortex
is a beacon
as are our toes.
You and I
are a river of light
that pours
and gleams
in
the
blue-black
snows.

We are perfect
as the tooth
of a squirrel!

—Lima-Huancayo railroad, Peru

40

POETICS

YES! THERE IS BUT ONE
POLITICS AND THAT
IS BIOLOGY.
BIOLOGY
IS
POLITICS.
We dive into
the black, black rainbow
of the end
unless we spend
our life and build love
in creation of
what is organic.
The old views
(worn and blasted)
are a structure
of death.
Our breath
IS
TO
SERVE
THE ULTIMATE
beauty
of ourselves.

ANTECHAMBER

for Larry Littlebird

The Portuguese Man-o'-war and the Jack Sail-by-the-wind are colonial jellyfish. Each organism is comprised of numbers of specialized individuals reproducing, hunting, and feeding together as a single being.

1.

I
KNOW
NOTHING
ABOUT
BOATS.
What I do know
is organisms:
THE
CELLS
and
BEINGS . . .

And I tumble
in the flashy silence

THAT I LIGHT WITH SELVES

and look for music

WHILE I MOIL UP

around the whirl I make.

This is not a carved wave

or the boundary of a bubble

nor even, sweetly, is it
a Jack Sail-by-the-wind
or Portuguese Man-o'-war.

(I mean those colonial beings,
Medusae clusters
in all their beauty.

We're like them too.

They're us!)

             Some say
          we're every thing.

                         Whatever that means . . .

  CERTAINLY WE'RE DARK FLESH MUSIC
       LAYING OUT A SHAPE

             with Luck
          for outrigger
       and our brain for keel.

_____

                DO
               YOU
              KNOW
               WE
            CROWDED
          ON THE LAND?

  DO YOU KNOW WE CROWDED ON THE LAND

                     (The black shapes in pansies
                        are imitating flocks
                       of nectar-drinking flies)

          —around the complex

complex brilliance

        of our feedback?

                AND
                WE
                BROKE
              THE SUBSTRATE

                          and made

            the shattered substrate

    and made

            the substrate shattered.

The forests
and the chaparral

                      are burned
                      and grazed
                      and fenced

            in imitation

of our selves.
            And now a new
            holistic style

is the secret desire

                          in the strongest

            smile.

We wish

to lure
perceptions
that make
our being

together
into constellations

like patterns in jade

and waves of stars

that sail through
black velvet

BUT

we're crumpled creatures

that move in helixes

and hurl out

strong

and hungry

loves.

———————————————————

WE'RE
RAINBOW-COLORED
KNIGHTS
IN SPASTIC BOATS

UPON A WHIRL-
POOL.

Each system

                                     that we build

        dissolves itself

                  confutes
                  its being

                              in its
                           completion.

                Each heiress
                that we kidnap

                        brings

her father's army

                on

                                  our heels.

                Surely

                          it is
                          time

    to think
    this out

                and put

                      the wings,

                    the pearl encrusted
                       wings, with
                      faces on each
                         feather

and wings upon

                         each face

                                        on every feather

                      on our brow.

                          We
                          are

                       OPALS

              AND BLACK SILHOUETTES
                   OF BUFFALOS

and laughing

                       aching

                                  galaxies

                      of meat

          and breath
          and life

                      bypassing

                                     death

                          50

in the rippling
                    of

                              an

                                   aeon.

───────────────────────────────

              THIS BOOK IS FAIRY STUFF.
                       It has

a radiance

                    and trembles real

          in sheens
          of light.

                                        The hands
                                        that wrote
                                           it hang
                                        in space

                    as shining freckled
                         APPLES

              in the boughs

                              of time

                    where the breeze
                         of luck

     is plucking

                    at the trunk.

                         51

WE'RE

INSTRUMENTS

THAT

PLAY

ourselves.

"What weapon
has the lion
but himself?"
asks

Keats.

AND
OH

within the cloud
of what there is
we're just as free.

FLESH

plays itself

and states

that it is meat,

viande,
and flesh
and
free

52

for
being
selves
if spoken to
in the language

        that it understands.

     WORDS
      &
     groans

like vertebrae

      are real.

     Every thing
     at all times

is on the verge

          of
        liberation;

    MUSCLES

  crackle

       when they loosen.

WE'RE
RAINBOW-COLORED
KNIGHTS
IN SPASTIC BOATS

53

UPON A WHIRL-
POOL.

We're
chunks
of opal
carved from ivory.

We're jellyfish

reflecting

light

in choppy
sunny
seas.

Tendrils
hang
down
from
us
and
stun
and
grasp
a
fish.

Sing Love! Ho Love!
It has lasted
a billion years.

Hey nonny!

Alladay!

Alladay down!

       Away with the frown

   and up

              with the eyelids.

—————————————————

WHEN
WE
PLACE
THE
VELVET
SADDLE BLANKETS
ON
OUR
SELVES
AND
SMILING
lie down to sleep
too often

and grow crazed

          with laziness

  we do not see

      in truth

         it's fear

    that pulls us back

55

and makes us drowsy

          AND REMOVES US

               FROM THE FRONTIER.

      For
      what

      we
      touch

   is shattered

      and all

              a-whirl and that's
                the way
                it is.

     WHEN NECKS HUNCH
     and shoulders turn
     to armor

we're like dogs
and cattle

     in our kennels

        and corrals

     BUT
     THE WASH
     AND CHOP
     is like

56

it always was.

                    WE CAN
                      SWIM
                        in it

        WE
        CAN

      STRETCH
      AND

       SING
       AND

       WALK
       LIKE

       FREE
      MAMMALS

or an eagle.

                The pulse
                  is all
                around,

    the only problem

       is that it's in

                    our image.

     The shattered substrate

imitates the shape

                                        of our

primordial behavior.

                    WE'RE BEAUTIFUL!

                                        We built

            too well

                too definite regarding

                                    what we think

            we
            are.

                    There's need for
                MUSCULAR IMAGINATION,
                        need
                        for

muscular imagination,

                                    in our motions

                not just

            imaginary
            minds

                    and magnificent

                    and constricting

                        58

                    but natural

                          models.

                       I
                      AM
                 A MAMMAL
                 PATRIOT.

            _____

                       I
                      AM

                 A MAMMAL
                 PATRIOT

        and LOVE

                                        all life

                    FOR
                    LIKE

            all life

                       I
                     move

                              in an expanding
                                          helix

through the waves
and fields
and forces

                          59

when

                      they're choppy

when

they're sleek
and soft:

        it
        is
        all
        the
        same
        for
        it
        is me.
I AM MY HAPPY

PAINFUL

                  body.

Whether cool or hot

    I

        am

             thought.

———————————————————————

WE ARE THE
ELECTRICITY

AND PADS
OF MATTER

AND
ALL

THE
SUBTLE

BILLIONIC
FIELDS

within
the
cataract
that
twists

through space.

WE
are
the whirlpool
and the jellyfish
and galaxy
and ape

of all our selves

inventing shapes.

We are baby lives
until we die
—locked
within some space—
until

61

some system wraps
itself around
our turning, twisting
motion
and tells us through
the limitations
that we are tied.

BUT still we know
that all conceptions

of boundaries

are
lies.

BUT still we know
that all conceptions

of boundaries

are
lies

and black flocks
of nectar-drinking
flies
are supping

at the yellow pansy's

cup,

are supping

at the

cup,

AND

ALL

THE GNATS
AT SUNDOWN

in the rosy
lovely light

are

COUSIN
ANGELS

catching
light

upon their wings

in the antechamber

of the night.

WE
ARE
MOVING
SIZELESS ROOMS
THAT
PUSH
AWAY

63

THE
DARK.

We're protoplasm

and

we're forests

made

of

sun
and air.

We're broken geodes filled with roses,
vats of honey in the depths of caves,
smiles of squirrels among the maple leaves,
moans of hungry dove babes,
red starfish imagining the waves,
cold
fingers
writing on warm sheets.
We're
white tigers

stalking

endless night.

We're all the loops

of selves

and ghostly elves

and trolls and giants

hurling
out

our
fronds

of
luck.

We're all
the energy

we drink
and chew

and suck
from sizelessness

to make

these behemoth

rooms,

to make

these behemoth

rooms.

JOIN
ME
HERE

65

                    IN
                   THIS
                  SPACE

        THAT WE

                                        INVENT

            FROM REAL STUFF

                  WHERE
                   WE

                  HAVE
                  NEVER

    laughed, nor danced

                  nor

                                    sung
                                  before.

                  WE'RE
            RAINBOW-COLORED
                 KNIGHTS
            IN SPASTIC BOATS
            UPON A WHIRL-
                  POOL.

                   I
                  AM

             A MAMMAL
             PATRIOT.

You know

that we

can walk.

YOU
KNOW

each challenge

issues

from
our
core.

We've

been
everywhere

before.

We're
physiques

of thoughts

upon a crowded
land,

and all the airiness
and aureoles
that we create

are
US

and all the airiness

and aureoles

that we create

are

US.

WE
ARE
MOVING
SIZELESS
ROOMS
THAT
PUSH
AWAY
THE
DARK

AND
all

the gnats
at sundown

in the rosy
lovely light

are

COUSIN
ANGELS

catching
light

upon their wings

in the antechamber

of the night.

FOR JOANNA

HOW BEAUTIFUL GRAVITY IS!
Can it get one high?
My
heart
is
a
sky

full
of

clouds

of blood

when

I run.

I grow
wise and
young

till

I

die.

CHANGER

for Russell

AT THE HOUR OF HIS BIRTH HE WAS
A WOLF-SHAPED CLOUD.
On his tenth breath he was a sea cave.
With the squirt of milk in his throat
he changed into a moon of Uranus.
When he first walked he was a butterfly landing
on a sailing ship.
Then
he was a pirate
and a sweating slave
at the oars. Soon
he was a sleek killer
whale.
Next
he became a buddha-like boulder
covered over
with mosses and nettles.
Next he was a shelf of fungus
on a cool tree trunk.
Then he became a giant elk
and a son of the wine god.
Next he became
a lake full of fish.
At last
he changed
into Proteus!

SONG

SURE, LET'S CELEBRATE THE BLACK SIDE
OF JOY. LET'S DROWN
the cup of cheer
in the barrel full of wine.
Let's see the wildflower's face,
all mauve and purple and bright yellow,
flattened by the pages
of a book—the spider
also pressed there
was once happy
chasing flies.

I worship all that's black.
To be alive's a shock
like listening to an angel,
or a fairy,
singing in a rock.

LISTEN LAWRENCE

LISTEN, LAWRENCE, THERE ARE CERTAIN OF US
INTENSELY COMMITTED
TO
a
real,
A REAL,
REVOLT! A REVOLT
that we only begin to
conceptualize as we
achieve it!
THE CONCEPTION
BEGINS SLOW
—as we do it—as we really do
it—as we make the revolution
with our bodies—our real BODIES!
OUR REAL BODIES ARE NOT DIVISIBLE
from the bulks of our
brother and sister beings!
We're alarmed by the simultaneous extinction
and overcrowding of creatures:
WE
BELIEVE
that the universe of discourse
(of talk and habit-patterned actions)
and the universe of politics
are equivalent!
THAT POLITICS IS DEAD
and
BIOLOGY
IS HERE!
We live near the shadow
AT THE NEAR EDGE OF THE SHADOW
((TOO NEAR!!))

of the extermination
of the diversity
of living beings. No need
to list their names
(Mountain Gorilla, Grizzly, Dune Tansy)
for it
is a too terrible
elegy to do so!

COMMUNISM,
CAPITALISM,
SOCIALISM,
will do
NOTHING,
NOTHING
to save the surge
of life—the ten thousand
to the ten-thousandth, vast,
Da Vincian molecule of which
ALL LIFE,
ALL LIFE
is a particle!

*

LISTEN, BELIEVE
ME,
none of us can afford to luxuriate,
if we care about the presence of life.
The
whole scene
IS ALL ONE DIMENSIONAL!
MARCUSE was right!
because he saw there is
only one, one-dimensional, planet-wide civilization
and realpolitik.
Unfortunately

75

it is modeled on one of the most
perfect aspects of our nature: THE DESIRE
TO GROW, TO WASTE, TO BREED, TO BURN UP,
TO EAT, TO TOSS DOWN, TO TEAR UP, TO FINGER
AND TWIST, AND TEASE, AND MAKE ALL
THINGS TERRIBLE AND DIVINE,
AND GLORIOUS! And we have
succeeded TOO WELL,
                    TOO WELL!
We are the most complete successes
the world has ever known!
                    POLITICS

is

part
and particle
of this horrific success, success
which is—in fact—an explosion that has
ALREADY OCCURRED. We have charred
the surface of the earth leaving behind
buildings which are cinders from the blasts
of oceans of petrochemicals!
Look, books and papers are
the fossil fuel explosion of trees!
LISTEN, LAWRENCE, this
is the same old politics! ANY, ANY, ANY
POLITICS
is the POLITICS OF EXTINCTION!

*

IT IS TIME FOR PEOPLE TO COME OUT OF THE CLOSET
ALL RIGHT,
            ALL RIGHT!
                    IT IS TIME FOR THEM
to come out of the closet—
OUT OF THE CLOSET OF POLITICS

76

and into the light of their flesh and bodies!
NOW
is
THE TIME
to learn to see
with the systemless system
—with the systemless system
like a Negative Capability—
of anarchist-mammal perception!
THAT'S BIOLOGY! Now is the time
to see that

it is our nature to be beautiful
and the destruction wrought by politics
is part of our beauty. Now we can learn
to see why it is our nature to go on with
this destructive politics. NOW WE CAN SAY:
LET'S STOP! LET'S STOP
THIS ENDLESS MURDER BY POLITICS!
LET
US
DO WHAT
WE CAN TO STOP
so very much useless pain!

It is our nature to overbreed and to kill!
But our nature has endless dimensions! We
can choose among them—we can reject,
we can reject the flowers of politics!

ACTION PHILOSOPHY

THAT GOVERNMENT IS BEST WHICH GOVERNS
[LEAST.
Let me be free of ligaments and tendencies
to change myself into a shape
that's less than spirit.
LET ME BE A WOLF,
a caterpillar, a salmon,
or
an
OTTER
sailing in the silver water
beneath the rosy sky.
Were I a moth or condor
you'd see me fly!
I love this meat of which I'm made!
I dive in it to find the simplest vital shape!

AH! HERE'S THE CHILD!!!

WHAT'S LIBERTY WHEN ONE CLASS STARVES
[*ANOTHER?*

STANZAS COMPOSED IN TURMOIL

The motile spirochete-like organism became more and more intimately associated with its aerobic mitochondria-containing amoeboid host.
—*Lynn Margulis,* Origin of Eukaryotic Cells

AND SO THE PARTS OF ME ARE DRAWN TOGETHER
BACK ALL THOSE BILLION YEARS, 3000
million years—No! Still more!
AND
FURTHER

back
and
BACK!

I am a cell!
I'm a cell within
a cell!

I'M
something
else.

I'm the Beatles.
I'm a MAMMAL
moving

BUT

WAY WAY WAY WAY WAY WAY WAY WAY

back
there

79

I'm part of you
as we explode out
of that black ball

into these realms
of fantasy! Hear
me tell you there

are fuchsias here upon
the table in that vase
upon the tartan, mohair drape

of blue, green, white, red.
—*And listen* to the sirens whooping
in the morning air!

SURE

THAT'S

THE WAY IT IS! IT'S NATION

TIME!

Time to wake up!
We are the Nations of our selves
drawn together. WE ARE IN DANGER

OF THE LOSS OF OUR DEEP

((OUR DEEP DEEP)) BEHAVIOR

IN THESE AWFUL CRUELTIES TO WHICH
we've brought (and created with)
our appetitions!

NOTHING MATTERS BUT MY LIBERTY!

WITHOUT MY LIBERTY, YOU'RE NOTHING, *NADA,*

ZERO!

(WHEN THOSE PARTS OF ME PULLED TOGETHER
THEY GAVE ME MOTILITY)
WHEN THE MITOCHONDRIA-BEING (Respirator) pulled
[into
his/hers/its protector
it found the universe and was joined by

a brother/sister organelle—the tail
(whip-mover—whip for all things are pain
and movement in this . . .)   THIS . . .)

LET'S GO! LET'S MOVE! ALL
IS BEAUTY; all is motion; let's move
ourselves within ourselves. KEEP IT

A-
LIVE!
YOU'RE GORGEOUS!

.
.
.

Your lovely soft brown skin I suck down my
gorge. Whether withered or maybe new. All

81

these years I do it. Time becomes real as
it becomes us. But you can drop it. DROP
IT!
DROP
IT!
WE'RE FREE! We're lib-
erated. We used our guilt to sharpen
senses. I can sight, sound, taste, touch, smell,
or gorge on you. Forge you into what you are as
you free me with your chains. Change is
what we're up to.—Why
I'm almost as mad about you as
YOU

ARE

ABOUT

ME
!

We're gold ostriches
running on the veldt of Time
looking for a place to stick our heads
while we flap our plumey wings.
WE'RE BACTERIA STUCK TOGETHER SINGING
(one-inside-the-other)
making motion.

PULSING / STREAMING

WHY, I CAN TELL YOU WE DON'T EXIST.
WAR, LOVE, REVOLUTION, DO NOT HELP
A BIT!

WE'RE THE LOST IMAGININGS OF INDRA'S NET
MELTED IN THE SOLID PULP OF NOTHING STUFF.

WE KNOW WHAT WE'RE DOING! LEONARDO DOESN'T
DO IT BETTER. THIS IS THE WAY IT ALWAYS IS
AND WAS. The Big Dipper
setting on the horizon edge
is our cup. We wake in the night
to look out on black cliffs in gray
fog. We've kissed each other ten
thousand times, nude upon the beach
after bathing in the icy waves
in mud-blue water while the kelp
is dragging at our legs.
The parts
of us joined
TOGETHER
long ago to bring
us to this place where
LOVE is the only answer
that

we've
got.

It doesn't help a bit.
It thrills and pains
as bad as ever.
STILL,
you free me,
you move me, you're
my motility, my freedom.
I'M
YOURS. It's
a mystery. It's hypostatized.

BREATH
HELPS

and your wrinkled smile,
and your toes running on the black
stones where the foam hits.

WE'RE BARELY HERE AND IT WAVERS, QUAVERS,
THRILLS, chills
me till I could scream and
fall apart again.

BUT WAY WAY WAY WAY

WAY WAY

WAY DOWN DEEP INSIDE
my core and yours
/which is everywhere and nowhere/
WE'RE

IN

DANGER

OF THE LOSS OF OUR DEEP

((OUR DEEP DEEP)) BEHAVIOR!

WE'RE ALWAYS THERE, ALWAYS AT
AN EDGE, ALWAYS TIP-TOEING
ON THE CRACK OF CRISIS.
OUR PHYSIOLOGY IS THE STATE OF CRISIS.

THE AWFUL
CRUELTIES

are us.
Are in-

distinguishable
from joys. Our sharing

eats our mammal brothers,
devours crustacean sisters

mating in the tide. WE BURN

INSIDE!
The white-tailed kite

hovers in the warming sun.
He looks for
the meadow mouse
with a silver star reflected in his eyes.

LET'S LOVE THE CRUELTIES

WE CRUELLY STOP

till we burst into self-consuming flames creating
us. HEY, we're in the car roar.
We're in the car roar. We're in the car roar.
Hey, we're in the car roar. We're in the car roar.
HEY!   HEY   HEY   HEY   HEY   HEY!

WE'RE   WE'RE

IN   IN

DANGER   DANGER

OF THE LOSS OF OUR DEEP, OUR DEEP BEHAVIOR.

I AM MY DEEP BEHAVIOR!

I'M MY DEEP BEHAVIOR!

I'M MY DEEP BEHAVIOR!

Dancing in my hungers!
Dancing in my hungers!

I AM ME-THOU-THEE! ME-THOU-THEE!

WE ARE THE NATION! WE ARE THE NATION!

WE ARE THE NATION! WE ARE THE NATION!

IN THE GLORY OF THE ACID RAIN WE ARE THE
[NATION!
In the rising buildings—Mammal Nation!
In the crumbling light we are the Nation!
WHAT WE ARE

INSIDE,

BELOW THE SOCIAL WHIRLING,

IS THE NATION, NATION, NATION,

IS THE NATION, MAMMAL NATION!

We're in danger.

THAT'S WHAT WE LOVE!

WE LOVE THIS DANGER!

WE ARE DEEP INSIDE!
WE ARE DEEP INSIDE!
WE ARE DEEP INSIDE!
WE ARE DEEP INSIDE!
WE ARE DEEP INSIDE!
WE ARE DEEP INSIDE!
WE ARE DEEP INSIDE!
WE ARE DEEP INSIDE!
WE ARE DEEP INSIDE
dancing in the car roar,
dancing on the beaches in the car roar,
dancing on the beaches in the car roar
in the Acid Rain, in the Acid Rain. No fear!
NO FEAR! NO FEAR! HEY! NO FEAR! NO FEAR! HEY!
NO FEAR!

San Francisco and Mendocino

RARE ANGEL

Rare Angel tracks vertically on the page and is Oriental in that way. The selves that comprise our whole being may play over this poem, as if it were a tape, and make prints and new codings. The selves can reach out and speak as the pages move past. The book gives birth to itself from the substrate by writing out muscular and body sensations which are the source of thought.

Rare Angel is about the interwoven topologies of reality. It reaches for luck—swinging out in every direction. It is about the explosion going on.

While we walk the city streets the old buildings sink into non-existence and the new buildings rise up. The flow of change is palpable and exciting. It is thrilling to be in this waste and destruction and re-creation. That is one of the sensualities of American culture. Our primate emotions sing to us in the midst of it. No one grants credit for the brilliance we burst in.

Whitehead says, "But when mentality is working at a high level, it brings novelty into the appetitions of mental experience. In this function, there is a sheer element of anarchy. But mentality now becomes self-regulative. It canalizes its own operations by its own judgements. It introduces a higher appetition which discriminates among its own anarchic productions. Reason appears."

—And *Rare Angel* appears like an organism with dark eyes, and bristly spotted fur and shining teeth. It is comprised, as our cells are, of Pleistocene hunts and toy umbrellas.

AND SO WE STRETCH OUT

(it is a muscular sensation
from the neck and shoulders
through the arm . . .

AND SO WE STRETCH OUT
and raise ourselves above our own
black factories.
And we are not in search of poetry but luck
that is ten-trillion Milky Ways
that make a molecule within our chest
or a billion feathered songs sung
from horseback on a bison hunt
WHERE BEAMS OF LIGHT
flash here and there
and make new colors out of dust
that we emit in Fields of Thought.

THEN I KNOW THAT I AM NATURE
where e'er I walk
or drink or think.
I AM THIS SWART PEARL
of Space
TURNED
INSIDE
OUT!

ALL STRANGE STRIPED
CREATURES SLITHERING
through the roots
grin and dance
TO
NEW MUSIC.
I am THEY or THEM!

AND

NOW
I am the man within this movie hall
where samurai are slashing with their swords
and flashlights play upon the concrete walls
and toilets smell like modern kitchens.

AND
I can NEVER let myself
go wild, for I remember
I AM ALL.
BUT NOW I AM CLEARER THAN THE CLOUD I EVER
[WAS.
NOW I AM HERE AND SMILINGLY BELIEVE
EACH THING.

SURELY YOU KNOW THIS IS ME. I CAN BE
told by my naked cock standing up
as I leap through space and fall
on everything I am. LIKE YOU,
WE
are all
and *everything*.

WOLF VIOLETS HOWL!

DREAMS OF OCTOBERS STRANDED ON
BLACK SHALE BEACHES.

Blackberries lying in snow.
Giant snapping turtles in hot, muddy water.
Fingers crossing the moon.
Scent of jasmine.
Tongue on flesh of cling peaches.

GRANDMOTHERS AND GRANDFATHERS FUCKING.
It is all as lovely

AS

A

PIECE
of fluff
THAT FLOATS.
.
.
.
.
.
.
.

93

.
.
.
.
.
.
.
.
.

THIS IS THE STUFF! WE ALWAYS KNOW IT IS.

THIS IS THE EXPLOSION
happening all
around us . . .

WE CREATURES
AT OUR CAVE LIPS . . .
(selves are caverns)
hang
down, draped
from ourselves
like waves,
or
stand up
like scarlet mushrooms
in the glowworm's light,

or swim
in cold
rivers underground
through the limestone
made of dots
formed in star clusters . . .

HELLO. HERE IS MY HAND I REACH TO YOU.
(It is something like a paw.)

THIS HUGE PIECE FLASHING BY
IS A CITY MIMING LIFE!

The sword slashes
through nineteen

95

bodies
—it is one
dream
of what
we want.

YOU

KNOW

ME

BECAUSE

I'M
WATCHING

YOU.

You have toes and breasts.

YOU COULD SAY I
wish to be
gentle, sweet, and lovable,
and that would be true, but it
would
stifle
all that matters

if it
became
a code
to live by

WHILE
all this

happens!

Faces peeping from rocks.
Clusters of nothing forming particles.
Rainbows over daisies.
Men watching eagles.
Coils of being turning
to new scents.

MESSAGES IN SEARCH OF SUBSTRATE.

Black zebras swallowing rubies.

Night hawks by barns.

AND THEN PICTURE THE FIELDS THAT STREAM
FROM THAT,
and the clouds they make—or squirms of energy

and relationship. I know
that it *cannot* be
distorted.
It all (as it explodes
or creates
itself—
or
anything)
is surely the messiah. I
fly by
without moving
in it.

Steady,

steady.

STEADY AS SHE GOES!

AND THEN I AM SITTING IN THIS WHITE TRUCK
AT THE CURB OF NOWHERE
where the rug is blood
AND
I
watch for you
because you'll know me.
And that is anthropoid or hominid
to always watch for ourselves
in the other's eye. To always
seek a mirror in hope that it will
FLATTER.
We
SCATTER
in the endless search

for trophies of the instant
because
they taste so sweet

but
it is
better
yet

to crack the scroll of time
instead!

— — — — — — — — — —

AND REACH INTO IT AS WE STRETCH!

WE

ARE
REAL

DRAGONS
OF OUR LUCK.

We swirl out what we are and watch for its return.

AND THE PHARISEES BRAND US WITH
TORTURED WORDS
in hope that they'll cause us anguish
for the grief we've hurled
(unknowingly
or
not)
at them. They drift
around like twisted demons.
MESSAGES OF SEXUAL JOY
we never asked for
(and
are
lies)
slither up and down the walls
in formless colors outlined
only
by the shapes of our desires.

WHILE THE WAR DRAGS ON
and little tufts of smoke
in passing eyes
remind us of the sizeless nearby battlefield.

•

Mutate into albinos.
Everything is cut
away
that was useless.
What's left
is
turned
to
new

101

nerves.

WE KNOW *THAT* IS HAPPENING TO US

((OR THE OPPOSITE))!

EVERY EXPOSURE

to

new condition

is our interwinding
with the welcoming messiah.
EACH
MOUNTAIN
is
a
breast
we fall upon.

IT IS NOT ENOUGH TO SAY THAT EVERYTHING IS US.
YOU ARE AS CLOSE AS MY TOUCH.
FUR.
MUSK.
MAROON PLUSH IN DARKNESS.
Scent of popcorn.
Rivulet of blood.
White buildings in the shroud of fog.
Amphipods in the icy tide.
Fronts of buildings with their back ends torn away.
Black man who sells me cola in his cave.
Angered
child.
Everything
winds in and out
in imitation
of our gut—
or vice versa!
It's more than we can know, except
by rubbing on it.
THERE
ARE
CONCEPTS
just beyond
our grasp
and we're always
at their edge,
when we care to be.
(And I cannot help but care
to be,
for that's my pleasure
and my claim
to what I see.)

TOUCH OF COLD WIND IN BRIGHT SUNLIGHT.

Smell of oil.

Dead fish on cracked ice

and

light *almost* trapped within the sun.

MEMORIES FROM ICELAND MIXED WITH
IMAGININGS OF INDONESIA.

GUN
KNIFE
LIFE
STUN
BUN
STRIFE
WIFE
FUN
STAR
TOMB
BOOK
FAR
WOMB
LOOK,
everything is flowing,
everything can see . . . All waves
have eyes!
Literature and life can melt together!

Crows float in air over douglas fir trees.

Thrones of carved jade in mountain caverns.
Smell of ponds in springtime.
(Darting of the pollywog.)
Daddy longlegs caressing in the moonlight.
Pressure of moonbeams on surf.
Red macaws sacrificed in clouds of copal incense.

Fractured surfaces of flint made into an edge.
Towers spouting oil.

105

Speeding tortoises of metal.
Eyes and nose holes moving on flat walls.

Miracles present themselves
for our benefit and we make
of them what we will.
WE
NEED
TO KNOW
that all these separations
make one thing,

or to learn about the illusion that we call *one*.
Or to see, like Kilroy, over the edge of something.

RAVEN'S FEATHER. EAGLE'S CLAW. EVERY
SONG EVER CHANTED
by the whale hunter
is a collector's item
and wafts like mountain fog
from node to node before becoming clouds.
EVERY
BACKWARD
LOOK
puts us in touch with sentiment,
and hurts less than peering forward,
for tomorrow is the shadow of today.
Even the blue jay
gloats over his stash
of brass buttons. See the octopus play
with the exoskeleton
of his prey.

The statement's convolution
confounds what is already done.

Bulldozed hillsides.

Scarlet flower bugles on the mountain top
overlook the graveyard.

Such elegant music when we make it
(for poets call it music)
surprises
US
in the act

of what we do.
The hand plays hide and seek
with the eye, and we grow
great brains
in honor of the game.
Then we dance and the music
follows at our footsteps
and we stop to listen
as it passes by.
WE
HEAR
THE MUSIC
OF
our selves!

Call it animal nature—or name it Civilization.

SPARROW HAWK SKULLCAP. LIGHTNING BOLT
THAT PASSES
THROUGH THE HAND.
WAVES OF CREATURES FLOATING
AT THE EDGE OF FIRE
dive into the air and bound
through space with grace
we nearly comprehend.

Bodies: brown and black and white all blended.
Hoofed and leaping.

TURQUOISE.

CHROME!

Berries and Packards all exploding, lined
with fur of force fields.

DESTRUCTION UNROLLED UPON THE PLEISTOCENE
where we stride in luscious comfort,
and love our children,
hug our pets,
experience
the
alchemy of being.

THE FEW OF US LIKE WAR CHIEFS
AND LOVE-GOD PRINCES
STAND ON THE PRECIPICE WITH FOLDED ARMS.
THIS
LIFE
has
been

nothing

109

for
me
but
pleasure.

The worst adversity
is only a length
I measure.
I direct creation of my bed of eider blackness
and drink the juice of apples
as I sup on flesh of crabs.
I
hold great minds
that lived before me
in my hands.
I KNOW THE MEANING OF THE POWER
THAT IS CHANNELED FOR ME. AND I
calmly watch the poisons
splashed across the land.

I HAVE CUT THROUGH THE HUMANE SURFACE
and I know all men and women
(and they
know me
for I
am them).
WE POUR FORTH OUR WANTS
in the center of this tornado.
Nothing can tear down
what we are
—we only color it with intellective lies.

I
WAS
RIGHT:
WE
ARE
LOVES AND HUNGERS!!!
—Delicate at moments, murderous and murmurous at others.
[Our

CRIES

are songs and howls
that we make into the sizzling air.

FOR KNOWLEDGE OF WHAT IS TRULY HAPPENING
(beyond our sense of fingertouch or ear)
we must read the walls
while they stand there
amidst the great unrolling,
and study the positioning
of garnets
on the boulder.

THE RETOPOLOGIZING IS RIGHT NOW! WE ARE
[WAVES

and Princes
in
the
surge!

LIKE ALL MEN AT ALL TIMES, WE ARE ELF
AND FAIRY FOLK!

HEAVY FOOTED AND LUMPISH OR LIGHT AND
DANCING ON THE FLOCCULENCE OF CLOUDS.
WITH DIM WITS OR EYES BRIGHT AND PIERCING,
the hungers are always all the same.
There is little change
except in the counting of the power
that flows to the lip of our ledge. The same
sacrifices evoke the new gods once again.
Zigzag knife or tracer bullet. Kisses made

between the sheets of a perfumed bed.
Little loving creatures there upon our laps
with big brown eyes.

NEW DRUGS
always in demand
to bring the loving god to hug us
as we dive to him and breathe in the embrace.

113

BUT
we are the Gods!
And not because we say so
in faustian paranoia. Or because
there is a wish to be.
The gift grew, and Luck
can push it further.

THE URGE TO DO IT FEEDS THE LUST TO GROW
BY MEANS OF SWIRLING
into spaces.
Silver towers in cold sea mist.
Severed arms.
Pink elephants and cherubim holding purple plastic flowers.

THOUGHT
is
a
muscular
sensation
pouring outward like
pseudopods with feathered hoofs.
Each hoof taps at the tacks
that press the scroll of the instant
flat upon the field of nothingness.

OH, HOW BEAUTIFUL!

BEAUTIFUL!

The wolf howl on the frosty night.

The rat upon the branch who eats
the cherry blossoms.

Grinning otter sleeping on the waves.

WE
cannot
be
sure
which constellations
open wide the fields like velvet drapes.
I only

watch. Driving
in it. Parking by
the gray curb
that is a universe
for the sensoriums
of
nematodes.
((Or parking by
the gray curb
that is a universe.))
Or
putting a black boot
in the rippling water
of a childhood day.
Or
hearing rain on an umbrella
in soundless space.